Animal
Babies

Books by YLLA

Animal Babies

The Duck

The Little Elephant

The Sleepy Little Lion

Tico-Tico

Two Little Bears

ANIMAL
BABIES

by YLLA

STORY BY **Arthur Gregor**
Designed by Luc Bouchage

HARPER & ROW, PUBLISHERS
NEW YORK, EVANSTON, AND LONDON

A lion roars in the jungle,
and even the leaves on the trees tremble.
But at home, lions look after their little ones
with much care. Here is a lioness who holds her cub
while he sharpens his claws on the wood.

Little lions hug their mother
to show how much they love her.

Their mother loves them too. She is proud
to see her little lions run about.

The kitten holds the cat on the floor. Puppy and dog
are pleased with each other, playing in the grass.

The hen must care for many little ones.
When her chicks get hungry,
she calls the farmer: kikiriki, kikiriki!
When he comes to feed them,
she looks to make sure
all of her babies are near her.

The ducklings follow the duck: quack, quack.
The little pig picks up his ears; mother pig does not stir.

Sheep wear coats of wool.
Young sheep, called little lambs,
do not yet wear a coat of wool,
only grown-ups do.
One day these three little lambs
will be dressed just like their parents.

The calf pushes her nose under the cow's chin.
The cow says: "Enough. Stop it now, little calf."

This mother horse shows her little colt how to stand up.
When he gets older, she will teach him how to trot.

A garden is most lovely with a pond in it,
a pond with willows surrounding it.
A pond is most lovely if a swan family
glides across the water. Little swans
must learn how to glide quietly,
must know how to open up their wings,
and when to keep them closed.
That is what their parents are telling them now.
One listens; the other turns away his nose.

Here is mother guinea pig with her young sons.
One nibbles on a lettuce leaf,
the other one has had enough to eat.

Mother rabbit listens.
No one is coming.
Quick, quick,
little rabbits have their meal.

The baby llama
obeys her mama
in what she may
and may not do.

The young camel
is a good son, too.
He goes with his mother
when she joins
the camel caravan.

An antelope family. First, little brother; then, sister; next, mother.
Father is last; he has big horns and watches over the rest.

Baby elephants, like this one,
stand close to their mothers
until they learn that
bathing in the river is great fun.

The giraffe is the tallest animal.
Even the baby giraffe is taller
than many an older animal.

Mother hippopotamus and her baby trot slowly and heavily; splish, splash, they are looking for a sunny spot.

Seals are happy in the water.
But at nursing time, seals prefer to be
where it is dry. That is why
mother seal has left the water:
to feed her baby daughter.

Monkeys can jump
from tree to tree,
hold on to a branch,
leap across the park,
jump down on a bench.
A little monkey
can do these tricks too,
and many other ones.
But a little monkey
is happiest
in his mother's arms.

Little tigers are full of mischief.
Lifting her head, the tigress wonders:
What are they up to now?

Up runs the youngest to show

his claws in his paws.

When the tigress walks away, one of her cubs
tries to catch her tail. She lets him play.
A few minutes more, and all little ones will be in bed.